Fishy Feelings

Written by Marvin J. Szukalowski

Illustrated by Matthew Forgrave

Edited by Brandy Thomas

Layout: Stacey Willey, Globe Printing, Inc. Ishpeming, MI

ISBN 978-0-9914955-0-4

Library of Congress Control Number: 2020921479

Aviva Publishing, 2301 Saranac Avenue, Lake Placid, NY 12946

Printed in the United States of America

To purchase additional books, please visit our website at: FishyFeelings.com

or email: marv@fishyfeelings.com

AViVA
PUBLISHING
New York

For Lily and Mason
"May you always find healing when you talk about your feelings."

Hello Minnows, my little human friends! Let's jump in the water because it's time to begin...
We are very much alike you and I, sometimes we laugh and sometimes we cry...

SUNFISH

I'm Sonny the Sunfish and

I'm swimming on my way,

I want all others to know

how I'm **feeling** every day.

 HAPPINESS

BLUEGILL

Billy Gilly is crying dry drops because
he's feeling a little blue.
Just because you're a bluegill,
you don't have to be sad too.

"Let's school together so we can rule together.
We'll stop your boo hoo."

 DEPRESSION

RAINBOW TROUT

Look it's Rhonda the Rainbow
she's all colors in one.
She can swim with us, we've got work to be done.
We don't want to swim in circles
and point our fins and blame.
We like each other no matter our sizes, colors of our
scales, boy or girls, or for our names.
In life every day there's going to be
changes in the weather.
We can never forget that we are all the same and
have to swim and play together.

 EQUALITY

LARGEMOUTH BASS

Hello Larry the Largemouth Bass,
just listen he will talk to
EVERYONE as they swim past.
He talks so much that everyone is just wishing...
he'd use that big bass stripe
which is his ears to listen.
There's so much that we could be missing.

 UNDERSTANDING

BULLHEAD

I'm Bully the Bullhead and I just want to fight,
"You shouldn't point, push, or yell at me...
You need to talk to others about your anger,
because that's your only right."

 BULLYING

ANGELFISH

I'm Angela the Angelfish and I'm here to remind you
always **love** the ones you've lost.
You need to talk about your **sad** feelings
don't just put them behind you.

 GRIEVING

SMALLMOUTH BASS

I'm Sam the Smallmouth Bass
and being green is my scene.
I don't need to have envy for others,
I just have to remember that
I'm only meant to be…. ME.

 JEALOUSY

SUNFISH SCHOOL

I'm Sonny the Sunfish
and I'm happy as can be,
because I've got a
bunch of new friends
swimming with me.
Come along
you'll see.

WHEN WE SCHOOL TOGETHER
WE RULE TOGETHER

CONTAGIOUS HAPPINESS

SMELT

I'm Smelly the Smelt a silver little fish,
I'm fast and I think I'm cute.
Sometimes I get a little gas in my tummy,
I just want to remind you to say,
"Excuse me," when you toot...

 MANNERS

PUFFER FISH

I'm Pete the Pufferfish
and if you don't want to get sick,
always wash your hands to a count of 20.
And that nose of yours...Don't Pick.

Wash your hands,
it won't take long.
Just sing out loud ......twice
"The Happy Birthday" song.

 HEALTHY HABITS

WALLEYE

I'm Wilma the Walleye.
My scales shimmer and are always Golding,
always be honest and don't steal.
It should only be your stuff that
you should be holding.

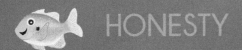 HONESTY

CLOWNFISH

I'm Chloe the fish named after a clown,
sometimes I'm the funny one. When you laugh
I turn your frown upside down.
I want you to know even though
I can stop the sad,
there are some days I'm hiding when
I'm feeling bad.

 SUPPRESSION

NORTHERN PIKE

I'm lke the Pike and every year
I molt and my teeth fall out.
It's quite a terrible sight.
If you want to keep your bite,
Brush your teeth after meals and snacks,
especially morning and night.

 HEALTHY SMILE

PHILIPPINE GOBY

I'm Felicia the Philippine Goby
and I'm tiny and spry.
All baby fish swim in a tight little school,
in a group and we're called fry.
We're not afraid of Whaleshark Willy,
Because we all swim together as one... SILLY.

 CONFIDENCE

GAR

I'm Gavin the Gar and we come
in all shapes and sizes,
just like different books on a shelf.
We have to remember that no matter how we look,
in this world we have to just be…OURSELVES.

 INDIVIDUALITY

PIRANHA

This is Paula the Piranha and she gets so mad
....she could just BITE.
Use all the tools that you can to
calm down the anger in sight.
Breathe deep, count to 10,
think like a dog, cat, or a sheep.
Or just focus on taking in a breath
and letting it out, LONG and DEEP.

ANGER

WHALESHARK

I'm Willy and I'm a Whaleshark
and I grow as big as a bus.
We think all fish are tiny
and should be very afraid of us.
"Willy we're not afraid of you, as you can see since
we all joined...together, We all RULE!
You can't eat us, but from now on
we'll let you swim in our School."

 COOPERATION

SUNFISH SCHOOL

Wow, we've become a big family. All you humans
and our school have come together as one.
Just look at what you learned and we had
so much FUN…

WHEN WE SCHOOL TOGETHER
WE RULE TOGETHER

We all share the same feelings but at different times
and ways. Sonny showed us how to be happy and
how to have fun in our EVERY days.
Feelings that we get can fill up our
minds and spaces.
When we don't understand and
share them with others, it'll put a smile...
back on our faces.

 UNITY

Blank Fish

I'm a fish that swims in your mind and cannot hide.
I know that all of your feelings are very real.
I want you to color my body just the way that you
truly feel on the inside.

 COLOR HOW YOU FEEL

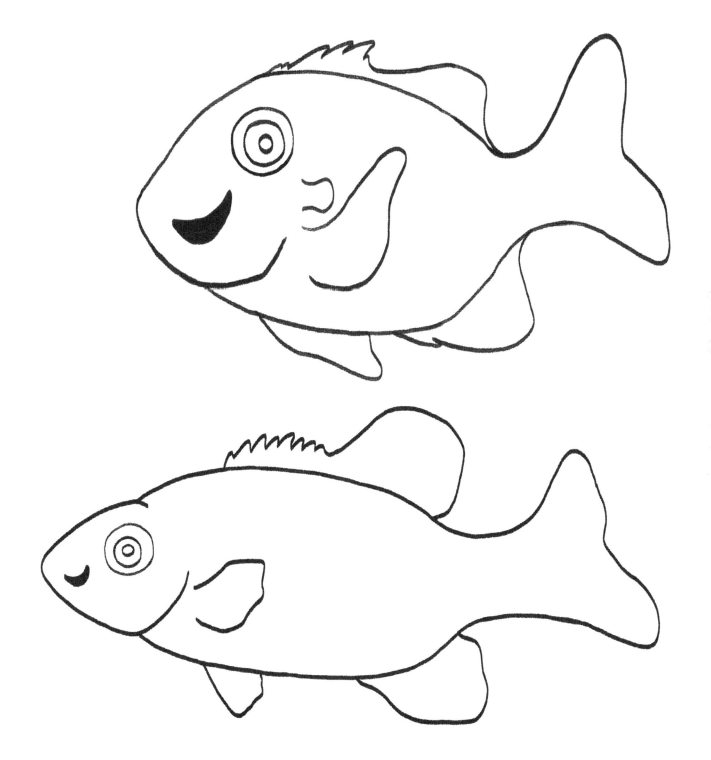

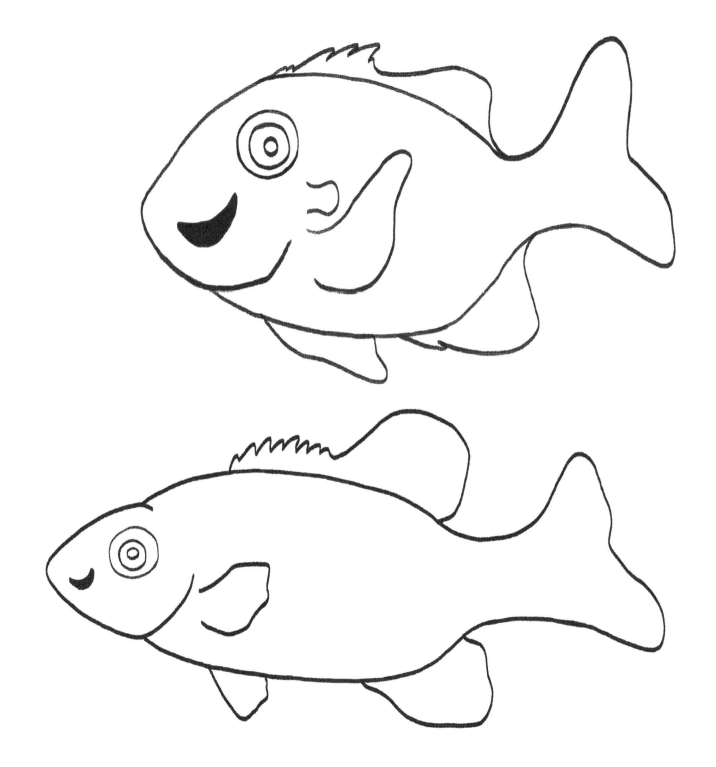

About the Illustrator:

Matthew Forgrave is an illustrator from Troy, Michigan, who has a bachelor's of fine arts degree in Illustration from Northern Michigan University. Matthew is passionate about storytelling and creating new worlds for his viewers to experience. His work focuses on childlike imagination and wonder, often containing environments full of life with many characters living in them. When Matthew isn't illustrating for work, he is usually drawing for fun and plein air painting, hiking and enjoying the outdoors.

About the Author:

Marvin J. Szukalowski grew up in and continues to grow in the Upper Peninsula of Michigan. The natural callings of the world play a critical part in the balancing of his life.

"*Fishy Feelings* was inspired by a conversation with a friend while out fishing. Years later I finally put some measure to the thought. I noticed one day that my grandson had emotions and tears but not the words to talk about his feelings. This melted me, and eventually lead me to look at natural emotions and feelings with words to help identify them. I'd like you to rediscover yourself with your, "Littles," while helping them understand it's OK to feel when they need a sense of direction.

Let the little fish icon and feeling at the bottom of every page allow you to naturally tell the child that their emotions are scalable, and fishy feelings are very natural and real."